Essays on Justice,

Volume 1

John Zehring

Essays on Justice, Goodness and Faith: Volume 1

Copyright 2019 John Zehring

Essays are reprinted with permission of The Christian Citizen, a publication of American Baptist Home Mission Societies.

Table of Contents

Introduction

Essays on Justice, Goodness and Faith

About the Author

Books by John Zehring

Introduction

I wrote a few books published by Judson Press, which led to the opportunity to write a few articles for <u>The Christian Citizen</u>, a social justice publication of the American Baptist Home Mission Societies led by visionary editor Curtis Ramsey-Lucas. That led to an opportunity to serve on their team as a regular writer. I embraced their mission statement: *Through <u>The Christian Citizen</u>, we seek to shape a mind among American Baptists and others on matters of public concern by providing a forum for diverse voices living and working at the intersection of faith and politics, discipleship and citizenship.* It is an honor to write for a publication like this. After a dozen or so essays on this theme, I now set out to gather some into a book on the theme of justice, goodness, and faith.

The title – <u>Essays on Justice, Goodness and Faith</u> – is inspired by Micah 6:8: *"He has told you, O mortal, what is good; and what does the Lord require of you but to do justice, and to love kindness, and to walk humbly with your God?"*

JUSTICE – how you treat people. To do justice is to open our eyes to those in need, especially those on the margins of society, and to be led to stand with and to speak for those who are oppressed.

GOODNESS – the craving to want to be a good person and a good nation, the basis of the first essay. I asked an eminent man of many achievements how he wanted to be remembered… what did he wish his legacy to be? He answered "I just want to be a good person."

FAITH – For those who proclaim "The Lord is my Shepherd," faithfulness to God comes first. Mother Theresa said "God does not call us to be successful. God calls us to be faithful."

This is Volume One. A prolific composer of classical music was asked which was his best symphony. He answered "My next one." I say that too for my articles and my books, hoping that the best is yet to come. I continue to write and, God willing, will create enough essays to make succeeding volumes.

NOTES ABOUT THIS BOOK

Scriptures used in the work come from the New Revised Standard Version, unless otherwise noted.

I have attempted to use inclusive language wherever possible in the words I have written, although I have not altered the author's reference to God as "he." I recognize that the Divine has no gender and for many it may be just as appropriate and accurate to acknowledge God as Mother or Father. Whichever pronoun is used, consider God as a loving parent.

If interested in books I have written, my website can be found by searching online for *John Zehring books*.

May these essays inspire you to grow in your doing of justice, wanting to be a good person, and deepening your faithfulness to God.

John Zehring

Make America 'good' again

I had the opportunity to share lunch with a man who was renowned. A major city newspaper featured a front-page story about him. A Renaissance man, he had a play running in New York City and a musical playing in Europe. He had CDs of his music, a book by Harvard University Press, two doctorate degrees, walls of awards and shelves of recognition.

During lunch at a Chinese restaurant, I was curious and asked him: "What do you want your legacy to be? In light of all your achievements, for what do you want to be known? How do you want to be remembered?" I will never forget his answer. It changed me. He said, "I just want to be a good person." At first that sounded underwhelming. As I thought about it, I realized how profound it was. What if everyone just wanted to be a good person? That goal could shape our lives and our world.

Goodness is one of the Apostle Paul's fruits of the spirit (Galatians 5:22). It is translated as generosity in the Bible's New Revised Standard Version, which makes sense because good people are generous people who give of themselves to the world. Paul's point is that, when we desire God's spirit to dwell within us, it changes what we want. It changes our goals. When God's spirit is invited in and treated as an honored guest, it changes us to want to be a good person.

A particular scenario and related quotation are sometimes attributed to French writer Alexis de Tocqueville. It is said that he was curious about what made America tick and made it a great nation. Legend has it that he considered America's harbors and fields, its vast world commerce, public school system, institutions of higher education and even its democratic Congress. Often credited to him is this conclusion: "Not until I went into the churches of America and heard her pulpits flame with righteousness did I understand the secret of her genius and power. America is great because America is good, and if America ever ceases to be good, America will cease to be great."

Maybe the logo on our red ball caps should read "Make America Good Again."

A warmly personal psalm that speaks about a follower's relationship with the shepherd, Psalm 23 concludes with the verse "Surely goodness and mercy shall follow me." Consider for a moment the meaning of *follow me*. Perhaps a deeper meaning is found in the words. What follows you? The waves that follow a boat are known as a *wake*. People speak of being "left in the wake." The wake of a boat can extend for miles behind and fans out to the sides. Look down from the airplane view and you can hardly see the boat traversing, but you can spot the long and wide wake following.

What if this phrase could also mean that we leave goodness and mercy behind us in our wake? When the Lord is your shepherd, being a good person and giving grace to others flows out of you and trails behind in your wake wherever you encounter people. Now the emphasis is not so much on what you get from the Shepherd. Now the emphasis is on how you radiate as a candlepower of one when God's inner light dwells in. That changes your life goal and inspires you to "just want to be a good person."

May God grant that we desire to be good people and a good nation.

Published in The Christian Citizen November 22, 2017

Is the universe still on the side of justice?

Principle number six of Martin Luther King Jr.'s Six Principles of Nonviolence is *"The universe is on the side of justice."* Is that still true? It sure does not feel like it. It didn't feel like it in King's day, and it doesn't feel like it today. If injustice were a market index, its stocks would be soaring.

Racism, getting worse. Policies, laws, rhetoric and politics favor with intensity the upper 10 percent at the expense of everyone else. The glass ceiling for women grows thicker. Safety nets for our most vulnerable are developing holes through which a tractor-trailer could drive. Fences rise and gates close to those named on the baseplate of the Statue of Liberty. Welcome and inclusion of LGBTQ people appear to be making giant strides in reverse. Climate change escalates geometrically, while foxes are placed in charge of hen houses designed to protect and care for God's earth. Leaders blatantly place ego, partisan rewards and self-interest ahead of the common good. It feels like the moral arc of the universe is bending the wrong way.

King reminded that it will take a long time, as it took the Israelites a generation to reach their Promised Land. *"We've got some difficult days ahead,"* King told the sanitation workers four years after he won the Nobel Price for Peace and the day before he drew his last breath at the Lorraine Motel. *"But it really doesn't matter to me now, because I've been to the mountaintop. And I don't mind. Like anybody, I would like to live a long life—longevity has its place. But I'm not concerned about that now. I just want to do God's will. And He's allowed me to go up to the mountain. And I've looked over, and I've seen the Promised Land. I may not get there with you. But I want you to know tonight, that we, as a people, will get to the Promised Land. And so I'm happy tonight; I'm not worried about anything; I'm not fearing any man. Mine eyes have seen the glory of the coming of the Lord."*

In spite of violence, death, struggle and ugly injustice, King held to his principle: *"Nonviolence believes that the universe is on the side of justice. The nonviolent resister has deep faith that justice will eventually win. Nonviolence believes that God is a God of justice."* Underline the word *believes* in King's principle. Nonviolence believes that the universe is on the side of justice. Even when it feels like we are taking multiple steps backward for every one step forward, we, as Christians, cling with hope to that belief as well.

Perhaps King's namesake, Martin Luther, famously said, *"Here I stand."* Well, here we stand as God-centered people. Here we stand for agape—for love—for desiring what is in the highest and best interest for others, even our enemies. Here we stand for peace and the safety of all people, no exceptions. Here we stand for forgiveness, compassion and grace, which we give to others, even when it is costly. Here we stand for light, knowing that the darkness will not overcome the light. Here we stand for justice for everybody.

King taught that *"Injustice anywhere is a threat to justice everywhere."* Here we stand with Jesus, as he stood with all the Samaritans of the world. While it's neither a popular nor comfortable thing to do, we choose to stand with him, as he stands for those most out of favor with the world.

We will stand with and speak for those who are despised, marginalized and neglected—like Jesus did, like Martin Luther King Jr. did, and like Paul did, as he held that *"There is no longer Jew or Greek, there is no longer slave or free, there is no longer male and female; for all of you are one in Christ Jesus"* (Galatians 3:28).

Financial investors are warned about market psychology that makes decisions based upon emotions felt when a market experiences gains or loses. Do not try to time the market, investors are advised. Rather, make your choices based upon long-term goals and hang in there through bull and bear markets. So, too, with Christians invested in the belief that the universe is on the side of justice. Through past advances, present declines and hope for gains in the future, here we stand to be a small critical mass who hold the deep faith that justice will eventually win.

Published in The Christian Citizen January 15, 2018

On being 'repairers of the breach'

People of faith are led to fix things that are broken. That is the message from Isaiah: "Your ancient ruins shall be rebuilt; you shall raise up the foundations of many generations; you shall be called the repairer of the breach, the restorer of streets to live in" (Isaiah 58:12).

Oh boy, were things broken in Isaiah's day! When Solomon's boy Rehoboam took over the united kingdom, he messed up everything he touched. He favored the rich; taxed the poor; ignored his advisors' plea to speak to people in a civil tongue; mistreated women; had a stunningly low approval rating but didn't care because he played only to his inner base of supporters; polarized his nation; enjoyed conflict; did not welcome strangers and foreigners; and sought not what was best for the whole but for his own self-interest. He was the worst leader in the nation's history.

The people said, "We're out of here." Ten of the 12 tribes took their marbles and headed north to form Israel. The two tribes that stayed behind formed Judah. Israel, the Northern kingdom, was taken by the Assyrians, who took the people into captivity. Judah, the Southern kingdom, was conquered by the Babylonians. The temple was destroyed and most of the people were forced to live in exile, where they sang the hauntingly sad song "By the rivers of Babylon—there we sat down and there we wept when we remembered Zion" (Psalm 137:1).

We're talking generations here. No light at the end of the tunnel. The people who once flourished in unity in the land of milk and honey were now no better off than they were when their ancestors were held in bondage in Egypt. And they wanted to know: What did we do wrong? Where is Yahweh? It does not make sense to us! It feels like evil is winning.

Isaiah's job description was to help people to make sense out of bad things that were happening and to call them to faithfulness to God. That must come first. The genius of Isaiah was that he knew that if a person was faithful to Yahweh, then they would respond with care for the poor, for the oppressed and for all those whom society rejects and avoids. If a person were faithful to God, then she or he would feel led to fix that which is broken.

When things are not going well, people tend to do more of the same thing. In Isaiah's case, the people engaged in more religious practices, such as fasting. The same could be said for other religious practices, then and now. Isaiah told them, "Such fasting as you do today will not make your voice heard on high" (Isaiah 58:4). Something different was needed. So what was needed? Isaiah put it in the form of a question: "Is it not to share your bread with the hungry, and bring the homeless poor into your house; when you see the naked, to cover them?" (Isaiah 58:7).

That has a familiar ring to it, from Matthew: "For I was hungry and you gave me food...I was a stranger and you welcomed me, I was naked and you gave me clothing... As you did it to one of the least of these who are members of my family, you did it to me" (Matthew 25:35–40).

Jesus and Isaiah are on the same page: Faithfulness to God leads to fixing things that are broken: broken spirits, broken hearts, broken lines of communication, broken people, broken systems, broken breaches and levees.

Do you remember the pictures after Hurricane Katrina of the broken levees in New Orleans? And recently in Texas, Florida and the Caribbean? Broken levees are metaphors for so much of what is broken in our time—symbols of all that has gone wrong in our nation's priorities pouring through the broken levees of neglect of the poor, racism, social inequalities and an economic system that favors the few at the expense of the mass. Our generation is becoming swamped with broken levees in climate change, in education, in safety nets for those unable to care for themselves, in care for the elderly, in health care, in addiction, in abuse, in denial of equal rights to LGBTQ individuals, in opportunity, in compassion and in hope.

Do you remember the pictures of the waters breaching the beaches at Fukushima, Japan, or in Puerto Rico? Those waters, too, serve as metaphors for so much that needs fixing in political leadership and governance, in journalism, in using nonviolent methods for resolving conflict and in the honorable treatment of Muslims, Mexicans, Medicaid recipients and everyone else who might not look like us.

The levees are breaking and covenants are breached. I can think of some to blame. But the Bible does not say *blame*. It says *repair*. Why should we expend energy in blame that we can expend repairing the breaches?

I wish there were instructions that could tell how to fix the breaches of our time that are bursting and broken. But Isaiah did not prescribe instructions on how to repair the breaches, restore the streets or fix broken levees. What Isaiah did provide was encouragement to his troubled nation, and perhaps to ours, too, to be good, to be faithful to God and then to fix things that are broken for people who are hurting.

Margaret Mead said, "Never doubt that a small group of thoughtful, concerned citizens can change the world. Indeed, it is the only thing that ever has."

We, in our churches, are a critical mass—small communities of faith who have the audacity to believe that we can accomplish things far bigger than what you'd expect from groups our size. We believe that the power behind us is greater than the task ahead. Let us want to be good, to be faithful to God and to fix things that are broken. And then, perhaps someday, it will be said about us that we were repairers of the breach.

Published in <u>The Christian Citizen</u> February 5, 2018

Our call to carry on unfinished work

April 4 marks the 50th anniversary of the assassination of Martin Luther King Jr.

Amos' prophetic words were a favorite text and life theme for King right until that fateful day in April: *Let justice roll down like waters, and righteousness like an ever-flowing stream* (Amos 5:24). Justice is care and advocacy for those on the margins—those least able to advocate for themselves and those with the least power, least voice, least security and least wealth. One of the finest translations of the word for *righteousness* is "right relationships." Let the care and advocacy for those on the margins roll down like waters, and right relationships like an ever-flowing stream. King lived and died so that men and women might do justice and pursue a right relationship with God and with every man, woman and child.

When King accepted the Nobel Prize for Peace on December 10, 1964, he questioned why the prize was being given for a work that was unfinished. "I must ask why this prize is awarded to a movement which is beleaguered and committed to unrelenting struggle; to a movement which has not won the very peace and brotherhood which is the essence of the Nobel Prize," he said.

In the same speech, King later said, "I still believe that we shall overcome."

Four years after the Nobel Prize, the work remained uncompleted, and the struggle felt like pushing a bolder uphill.

"We've got some difficult days ahead, he said on April 3, 1968, in Memphis to sanitation workers on strike. "But it really doesn't matter with me now because I've been to the mountaintop. And I don't mind. Like anybody, I would like to live a long life. Longevity has its place. But I'm not concerned about that now. I just want to do God's will. And He's allowed me to go up to the mountain.

And I've looked over, and I've seen the Promised Land. I may not get there with you. But I want you to know tonight, that we, as a people, will get to the Promised Land. And so I'm happy tonight; I'm not worried about anything; I'm not fearing any man. Mine eyes have seen the glory of the coming of the Lord."

The following day—April 4, 1968—King walked out the door of Memphis' Lorraine Motel and drew his last breath. He did not get to the Promised Land, and the work remains unfinished. But what powerful foresight that we shall overcome someday. *Someday justice will roll down like waters, and righteousness like an ever-flowing stream.*

Giacomo Puccini, the Italian composer, wrote a number of famous operas, including "La Boheme," "Madame Butterfly" and "La Tosca." In 1922, he was stricken by cancer while working on his last opera, "Turandot," which many now consider his best.

Popular legend notes that Puccini told his students, "If I don't finish 'Turandot,' I want you to finish it for me."

Shortly afterward, he died. Puccini's students studied the opera carefully and, after considerable work, completed it. In 1926, the world premiere of "Turandot" was performed in Milan with Puccini student Arturo Toscanini directing.

Legend tells how everything went beautifully, until the opera reached the point where Puccini had been forced to put down his pen. Tears ran down Toscanini's face. He stopped the music, put down his baton, turned to the audience and announced, "Thus far the Master wrote, and then he died."

Silence filled the opera house. It was an unusual, uncomfortable interruption. Then Toscanini picked up the baton again, smiled through his tears and exclaimed, "But the disciples finished his work." When "Turandot" ended, the audience burst into thunderous applause. That performance became one of the most memorable in the distinguished history of opera.

Toscanini's words provide a valuable reminder of who must finish the work of Martin Luther King Jr.: us. We are needed to finish the work so that, someday, *justice may roll down like waters, and righteousness like an ever-flowing stream.*

Justice is not yet rolling down like waters. When it comes to justice, right relationships and the stewardship of this Earth, which is the Lord's, there are times when it feels like our nation is making giant strides in reverse. The work is unfinished and people of God are needed to finish the work, to speak for and stand with those whose voice is powerless, to advocate for those on the margins of society, to share our plenty with those who do not have enough, and to care for those who are hungry, naked, in prison, undocumented, victimized and discriminated against.

Moses stood atop the mountain and viewed the Promised Land, but he knew that others would have to carry on the work he could not complete. Jesus, from the cross, knew that others would have to carry on the work he could not complete. And so, too, King stood atop the mountain and viewed the Promised Land, and he knew that others would have to carry on the work he could not complete. The work remains unfinished. And while we might not get to the Promised Land either, like Puccini's disciples, we are called as Christ's followers to help finish the master's work, especially to those whom the King called "the least of these who are members of my family" (Matthew 25:40).

Published in The Christian Citizen April 4, 2018

Why all people of faith need Yom Hashoah

Editor's note: Yom Hashoah is marked on the 27th day of the month of Nisan, a week after the seventh day of Passover, and a week before Yom Hazikaron, a day commemorating Israel's fallen soldiers.

All people of faith need Yom Hashoah, the day each year when the Holocaust is remembered, because next time—and there could be a next time—it is possible that we might be on the wrong side.

In English, *Yom Hashoah* is commemorated as "Holocaust and Heroism Remembrance Day."

According to the U.S. Holocaust Memorial Museum's online *Holocaust Encyclopedia*, the "Holocaust was the systematic, bureaucratic, state-sponsored persecution and murder of six million Jews by the Nazi regime and its collaborators."

"*Holocaust*," the website continues, "is a word of Greek origin meaning 'sacrifice by fire.' The Nazis, who came to power in Germany in January 1933, believed that Germans were 'racially superior' and that the Jews, deemed 'inferior,' were an alien threat to the so-called German racial community."

Others who were targeted "because of their perceived 'racial inferiority' included Gypsies, the disabled and some of the Slavic peoples [Poles, Russians and others]," according to the website. Others, too, the website says, "were persecuted on political, ideological and behavioral grounds, among them Communists, Socialists, Jehovah's Witnesses and homosexuals."

I served as senior pastor of a church in a state capitol and, as such, was invited to become a member of the board of directors of the state's Holocaust Center. Around the table and beside me sat Holocaust survivors—men and woman with tattoos on their arms, not by choice, identifying them as Jews and marking them for extermination in concentration camps. All had lost homes, possessions, life savings and beloved family members.

They were the few who survived the camps.

In the international news came reports from a nation ruled by an ego-driven authoritarian leader that ethnic cleansing and genocide was being practiced. I wondered what lessons we learned from the Holocaust that could apply to new threats. As a pastor, I was curious about what my congregation was doing during the time of Adolf Hitler. I wondered what it should have been doing. I was haunted by questioning what I would have done.

"When you were in the concentration camps, what do you wish our churches would have done?" I asked a Holocaust survivor.

He responded: "What we hoped was that someone would know what was happening to us, would care and would remember us."

Just as some people deny that the Earth is round or that humans really landed on the moon, some deny that the Holocaust happed. They are known as *deniers*. "Fake news," they claim. But it really happened, and the horrors were brutal. In the end, Holocaust survivors were liberated by Americans and allied troops known as *liberators*. Every Yom Hashoah, liberators are thanked.

According to A Teacher's Guide to the Holocaust website, Lieut. Col. Lewis H. Weinstein, chief of the liaison section of General Dwight D. Eisenhower's staff, told of the April 1945 day when liberators entered the concentration camps: "I saw Eisenhower go to the opposite end of the road and vomit. From a distance I saw Patton bend over, holding his head with one hand and his abdomen with the other. And I soon became ill. I suggested to General Eisenhower that cables be sent immediately to President Roosevelt, Churchill, DeGaulle, urging people to come and see for themselves. The general nodded."

Could it happen again? Genocide is happening today. According to Genocide Watch, genocide emergencies are occurring in Syria, Sudan, Iraq, Central African Republic, Myanmar and Nigeria. Worries are growing in other nations.

Even more alarming, in the United States, demonstrations occur where swastikas and Confederate flags wave to signal a frightening hatred and blind patriotism to wrong values. Consider early warning signs of Fascism, as listed in <u>Washington Monthly</u>, to see if they are creeping into American culture, even at the highest levels of leadership:

"powerful nationalism" ("my country first");
"disdain for human rights;"
"identification of enemies as a unifying cause;"
"supremacy of the military;"
"rampant sexism;"
"controlled mass media" (claims of "fake news" about reports that name the evil);
"obsession with national security;"
"religion and government intertwined;"
"corporate power protected;"
"labor power suppressed;"
"distain for intellectuals and the arts;"
"obsession with crime and punishment;"
"rampant cronyism and corruption"; and
"fraudulent elections."

According to A Teacher's Guide, On April 12, 1945, Eisenhower wrote the following in a letter to Chief of Staff George Marshall: "I have never felt able to describe my emotional reaction when I first came face to face with indisputable evidence of Nazi brutality and ruthless disregard of every shred of decency. I visited every nook and cranny of the camp because I felt it my duty to be in a position from then on to testify firsthand about these things in case there ever grew up at home the belief or assumption that the stories of Nazi brutality were just propaganda."

The Holocaust is not "fake news" and must never happen again. But it could. There are early warning signs and threats.

Next time—and God forbid there is a next time—the following might be true:

The VICTIMS might not be Jews but could be Muslims, Mexicans, Medicare recipients, LGBTQ individuals or others whom our country's leaders have named as groups of people they consider unworthy.

The LIBERATORS might not be us and our allies but other nations upon whom the mantle of moral and humane responsibility has fallen.

The PERPETRATORS might not be Nazis. In the worst case, the perpetrators next time might be us.

We as people of faith need Yom Hashoah. We must never forget so there will not be a next time. Let us hold to the view that every individual is a unique wonder, created by God—never to be repeated in all of history—and, thus, should be treated as God's most sacred creation. In the name of everything that Jesus taught about what God desires, let us remember the Holocaust and pledge to speak for and stand with any person who is oppressed.

A Prayer for Yom Hashoah

Almighty and Merciful God, King of the Universe,

We pause to remember. This is not something we enjoy. It is something we must do. We have a duty to remember your beloved children and the suffering and death they experienced. We have a sacred obligation to tell the story—and to pray that such evil may never again walk the face of the Earth.

We confess that there are times when the idea sneaks into our minds, questioning, "How could you let it happen? These were your children." Then we remember that you never said there would not be the valley of the shadow of death. You never said that your table would not be in the presence of enemies. What you said was that, in our valleys of dark shadows, "thou art with me."

Be thou our shepherd, and be present among us. Eternal God, you spoke to your people in Isaiah (43), saying: "Do not fear, for I have redeemed you; I have called you by name, you are mine. When you pass through the waters, I will be with you; and through the rivers, they shall not overwhelm you; when you walk through fire you shall not be burned, and the flame shall not consume you. …Because you are precious in my sight, and honored, and I love you. …Do not fear, for I am with you."

What fear they must have felt, O God, when enemies did surround them and seek them out, when the rivers did consume them and the fire burned their bodies—all because of who they were. It is beyond our comprehension, and we can only trust that you were with them in their valley of the shadow of death, and that they dwell in the House of the Lord forever.

Grant that we may pledge ourselves anew:

to be your agents of love, compassion and forgiveness;
to speak out against the oppression of all people;
to labor for peaceful reconciliation among all people;
to oppose injustice and wrongdoing;
to encourage one another and to build one another up;
to unite in our conviction that nothing like the Holocaust should ever happen again;
to teach our young about what happened and what can happen;
to live as children of God; and
to speak a word of hope and trust in You.

Let those of us who proclaim "The Lord is my Shepherd" serve as a critical mass to teach and to model your ways.

Today, we remember.

Amen.

Published in <u>The Christian Citizen</u> April 10, 2018

In God we trust

In God, whose word I praise, in God I trust.
Psalm 56:4a

I grew up in a church where a previous pastor, a century and a half before me, was responsible for the motto on our nation's money: "IN GOD WE TRUST."

His name was Mark R. Watkinson. Born in 1824 New Jersey, Watkinson became a Baptist minister. In 1850, he began to serve First Particular Baptist Church, a small church in Ridleyville, Pa. Ordained in 1851, he stayed at Ridleyville a few more years before going to serve First Baptist Church of Richmond, Va. Watkinson was in Virginia when the Civil War broke out and, in 1861, returned as pastor to First Particular Baptist Church.

They were troubling times, the depths of which we can hardly imagine as the country was divided, and no one knew how it would turn out. Watkinson felt that the Civil War was going to leave the country with a bad name because of brother fighting brother. So Watkinson wrote to Secretary of the Treasury Salmon P. Chase, suggesting that a motto that recognized God be placed on U.S. coins. Over the years, others wrote similar letters; however, according to U.S. Treasury Department records, the first appeal—and the one that made the difference—came in a letter dated Nov. 13, 1861, from the Rev. M. R. Watkinson of Ridleyville.

Watkinson wrote, in part: "Dear Sir: You are about to submit your annual report to the Congress respecting the affairs of the national finances. One fact touching our currency has hitherto been seriously overlooked. I mean the recognition of the Almighty God in some form on our coins. You are probably a Christian. What if our Republic were not shattered beyond reconstruction? Would not the antiquaries of succeeding centuries rightly reason from our past that we were a heathen nation?"

Watkinson proposed a motto on the coin recognizing God, arguing: "This would make a beautiful coin, to which no possible citizen could object. This would relieve us from the ignominy of heathenism. This would place us openly under the Divine protection we have personally claimed."

As a result, Chase instructed James Pollock, Director of the Mint at Philadelphia, to prepare a motto, in a letter dated Nov. 20, 1861: "Dear Sir: No nation can be strong except in the strength of God, or safe except in His defense. The trust of our people in God should be declared on our national coins. You will cause a device to be prepared without unnecessary delay with a motto expressing in the fewest and tersest words possible this national recognition."

Two years later, the director of the Mint submitted designs for a new one-cent coin, two-cent coin and three-cent coin to the secretary for approval. He proposed that upon the designs should appear either OUR COUNTRY; OUR GOD; or GOD, OUR TRUST.

In a letter to the Mint director on Dec. 9, 1863, Chase stated: "I approve your mottoes, only suggesting that on that with the Washington obverse the motto should begin with the word OUR, so as to read OUR GOD AND OUR COUNTRY. And on that with the shield, it should be changed so as to read: IN GOD WE TRUST."

Congress approved, and the motto IN GOD WE TRUST first appeared on the 1864 two-cent coin just three years after Watkinson wrote his letter from Ridleyville. Over time, the motto was placed on all U.S. coins and, in 1957, was added to our paper money.

Watkinson died in 1878 at the age of 54. His contribution of the motto on U.S. currency was largely forgotten until the 1950s, when research uncovered his role. In April 1962, a plaque was placed at Watkinson's church, now named Prospect Hill Baptist Church on Lincoln Avenue in Prospect Park, Pa. I was there that spring day as a teen in 1962. That was my church. I spent the first years of my life in Prospect Park, lived a block away from the church, was baptized there, went to church school there, headed up the youth group there, and have even preached there.

It's hard to grow up in the shadow of the origin of our currency's motto IN GOD WE TRUST without incorporating that motto into daily thoughts. Psalm 56 proclaims: "In God, whose word I praise, in God I trust"—a frequent phrase in the Psalms.

Consider a few others:

"I trust in you, O LORD; I say, 'You are my God.' My times are in your hand" (Psalm 31:14–15a).

"Trust in him at all times, O people; pour out your heart before him. God is a refuge for us" (Psalm 62:8).

"You who live in the shelter of the Most High, who abide in the shadow of the Almighty, will say to the LORD, 'My refuge and my fortress; my God, in whom I trust'" (Psalm 91:1–2).

"Commit your way to the LORD; trust in him, and he will act" (Psalm 37:5).

The message of the Psalms and the message printed on our money reminds us that you can trust in God. Watkinson felt the nation needed that message during a time that was possibly the most divided time on our country's history. Now, once again, polarization, divisiveness and partisanship wring goodness out of our nation. How urgently we need to hear once again that even in bad times—especially in bad times—our trust is in God.

Published in <u>The Christian Citizen</u> May 24, 2018

By the Golden Rule, torture is always wrong

The message is simple and clear: According the Golden Rule, torture is wrong. According to the Golden Rule, torture is always wrong. The Golden Rule is the highest moral principal of humankind. It is worthy to guide you in figuring out what is right or wrong.

According to Newsweek, "one out of every five countries" surveyed by Amnesty International maintains a "'significant' presence of armed groups" that have committed abuses. Further, 48 percent of Americans say there are some circumstances under which the use of torture is acceptable.

In 2014, the Senate Intelligence Committee issued a report documenting that, under the George W. Bush Administration, the torture inflicted was far worse than reported. According to an article in The New York Times: "The Senate Intelligence Committee…issued a sweeping indictment of the Central Intelligence Agency's program to detain and interrogate terrorism suspects in the years after the Sept. 11 attacks, drawing on millions of internal C.I.A. documents to illuminate practices that it said were more brutal—and far less effective—than the agency acknowledged."

And when candidate Donald J. Trump was asked if he would condone torture, specifically the practice of waterboarding, he answered, "Would I approve waterboarding? You bet your ass I'd approve it. In a heartbeat. And I would approve more than that. And don't kid yourself, folks. It works. OK? It works. Only a stupid person would say it doesn't work." To which Clyde Haberman in The New York Times—hardly comprised of stupid people—replied via headline on an opinion piece: "No, Mr. Trump, Torture Doesn't Work."

Whether or not many of the planet's nations practice torture, and whether or not the U.S. president or any of his agency heads might consider the benefits of torture, the practice fails the test the Mount Everest of human ethics found in the Golden Rule: *Do to others as you would have them do to you.* The Golden Rule is the peak of social ethics and the Everest of all ethical teaching.

Today you can look up any word or verse in the bible by computer in the blink of a second. A remarkable observation about the Golden Rule is that it is difficult or impossible to find even by computer because every single word is so simple. Ten of the 11 words have only one syllable. How do you find it by looking up *do* (2,678 results), *to* (21,000 results), *others*, *as* and so on? The highest moral principle known to humankind can be spoken with the simplest words in every language, and it is easy to remember. Children learn it and understand it, sometimes better than adults.

This Mount Everest of human ethics is found in every great religion on the planet, including:

Judaism: "What is hateful to you, do not to your neighbor."—Hillel

Confucianism: "What you do not want done to yourself, do not do to others."—Confucius

Islam: "Do unto all men as you would wish to have done unto you; and reject for others what you would reject for yourself."—Hadith

Hinduism: "Do naught unto others which would cause you pain if done to you."—Mahabharata

Buddhism: "A state that is not pleasing or delightful to me, how could I inflict that upon another?"—Samyutta Nikaya

Christianity: "Do to others as you would have them do to you."—Luke 6:31

If a planet full of human beings in their morality hold anything in common, it is the Golden Rule. It is interesting to note how many of the great religions and philosophers put it in the negative, as in "Do not do." Jesus of Nazareth put it in the positive, indicating that the faith he taught was not a religion of avoiding but a proactive religion of doing.

This highest stage of moral development, the Golden Rule, can proscribe a moral absolute of right and wrong, and that is:

By the Golden Rule, torture is wrong.

By the Golden Rule, all torture is wrong.

By the Golden Rule, torture is always wrong.

By the Golden Rule, torture is wrong, even if it appears to serve a greater good.

By the Golden Rule, those who inflict torture are wrong, those who condone torture are wrong, and those in high places who knowingly allow torture are wrong.

The Golden Rule is a fixed point of truth, recognized by humans throughout the world and throughout time and of every religion: *Do to others as you would have them do to you.*

I have failed at the Golden Rule. You have failed at the Golden Rule. My country has failed at the Golden Rule. By God's grace, let us pick ourselves up, extend grace to those who have failed, and march forward to the moral principle of how to live that is nearest and dearest to the heart of God, Yahweh, Allah, Buddha, Ahura Mazda, the Great Spirit, to humanists and philosophers, and to all who hope for a world in which the good, the right and the just triumph over the bad, the wrong and the unjust.

Published in The Christian Citizen April 24, 2018

Be honest: Why do you want your church to grow?

Looking for a new pastorate? Chances are astronomically high that the church profiles or job descriptions you pursue are prominently recruiting for a new pastor who will help their church grow and, especially, attract new young families. Growing the church has become one of the premier skills sought in new pastors. Today's currency for congregations: Can you bring them in? Can you attract new members, build attendance and increase participation?

The need is obvious. Charts of church membership look like a skier plummeting off a steep cliff. Church school enrollments break new records for decline. Sports and community activities now think nothing of scheduling their events for Sunday mornings, drawing away young families who feel bad about it, but you know, folks, that's the way it is today.

Choirs become depleted and regularly beg for people to join them, even those who cannot hum a tune. Church school teachers are an ultra-rare commodity, and with safe church policies encompassing every congregation, now two teachers are needed to replace the one who did it before.

Church giving is in regular and steep decline as members dwindle, and one more time, year after year, there are no raises for the staff, needed maintenance is deferred, and program funds are trimmed to nil. The fund-raisers which once filled in the gaps die a natural death as volunteers no longer have time, energy or willingness to commit to large-scale fairs, sales, dinners or auctions.

The clergy themselves try as they can to maintain a positive attitude but become disheartened and wonder, "Is it me?" Congregations wonder the same and fantasize about a dynamo in the pulpit who might restore their fortunes to the glory days gone by.

Clearly, most churches want to grow. Every church would love to see young families and new members streaming in the door. "We must be doing something right," they say when attendance rises. It feels good, fuels the budget and staffs the volunteer needs of the choir, educational program and committees. When attendance declines, the refrain instead is, "We must be doing something wrong. Maybe we need to get a new pastor, change our music or advertise in the newspaper." Herein lies a theological conundrum: Attendance is linked to feelings, mood, morale and a confirmation that something is either right or wrong.

We are desperate! (Though the church hopes this will not be too obvious!). We need money. We need people to fill all the empty seats. We need leaders. We need more choir members. We need more teachers. We need. We need. We need. We are needy. Any new prospective visitor stepping foot inside the sanctuary may be greeted by observers silently asking themselves, "How can we use you?" New attendees can smell this a mile away and it turns them off.

The fact of the matter is that your attendance growth or decline is linked more to the demographic shifts of your zip code than anything else. If your zip code is growing ten percent a year, you will likely see growth in church attendance even if you are flubbing everything. On the other hand, if your zip code is shrinking ten percent a year, you will likely see a decline in church attendance even if you produce the most spirit-filled, vibrant and inspiring worship services ever created.

In reality, growth and decline link significantly to demographics and culture. If the culture reflects a decline in membership-based organizations (churches, country clubs, teams, museums, musical organizations, etc.), recognize that good programming alone will not swim against the strong tide of the culture's inclination to avoid the commitment of belonging to an organization.

There are strategies your church can employ to build attendance and participation if it has the will and the willingness to invest, but first and foremost it must choose the right reasons for desiring growth. In other words, what is your theology of growth? Why do you want to grow?

Churches that have started enthusiastic campaigns to stem the tide of decline and bring in more people, so that the church will possess more of everything it wants, seem to burst with initial excitement and then fizzle out with few, if any, results. Perhaps it boils down to the intent. Is our motivation *us-directed* or *other-directed*? Us-directed campaigns are about meeting our needs, our wants, our budgets and filling our empty seats. Other-directed campaigns are targeted specifically toward meeting the spiritual needs of others.

People do not want to belong to a needy organization. They want to belong to an organization that meets needs! The moment a church shifts its attention to meeting their needs, it becomes spiritually-centered in offering in service to another that which the church possesses. Is that not a definition of ministry? Is that not the intent of Jesus' call to "Go ye into all the world…" (Mark 16:15 KJV)? It is not about our needs, but their needs.

The epicenter of building attendance and participation revolves around the God-like attitude of wanting to meet the needs of others. Your congregation meets the spiritual needs of participants better than any other human organization. Your church meets the needs of the whole person and recognizes that a person cannot be whole without God in his or her life. When a person is not whole, he or she is fragmented. For people whose lives feel fragmented, your church offers a pathway to becoming whole. The key question becomes, "How can we meet more of people's needs?" Hold high the banner declaring that your intention is first and foremost to meet needs.

To put this in theological language: People are lost and God wants them found. Or, people are seeking and you know in your heart that your church meets needs. Many of your people have testified so. Adopt the right reasons for growth: to meet the needs of others in your community. Then the tools, strategies and investments you choose will follow the right goals for the right reasons.

Published in The Christian Citizen, November 14, 2018

A "Me Too" movement is needed for emotional abuse

My mother, in her 70s and alone for many years, went to a dance with her girlfriends where a man asked her to dance. She was flattered that a man took notice of her and then later asked to see her again. She defended him to family and friends, months later, as he became pathologically controlling – so much so that she needed his permission to call her friends and then only if she told them how wonderful he was. "Tell them about me," he whispered firmly as he placed his ear against the phone to listen to the conversation.

Did he hit her? No, not physically, but he hit her with a two-by-four of emotional abuse. Would physical violence have been more abusive than his narcissistic, obsessive need to control which thrust its jealous hand into her soul and cupped it over her heart, smothered it, denied it breathing space and crushed its joy until it just could not beat another beat? He knew her vulnerability and her need and he exploited it. Emotional abuse is domestic violence.

Around the world, at least one in every three women has been beaten, coerced into sex or otherwise abused during her lifetime. Far more will be emotionally abused. Domestic abuse does not care about how much education you have, how well raised you were, how much money you've got, how successful you've been, what kind of person you are, where you live or where you go to church.

When I became Senior Pastor of a large church in an affluent community, I could find no resources in town for victims of domestic abuse. I asked leaders of the church where people could go. Their answer: "We don't really have that problem in our community." A few weeks later, our police chief told me that reports of domestic abuse increased 82% in the previous year. Help must be very easy to get and very accessible or it will not be used. Some churches have phone numbers for help on the inside of bathroom stalls in the women's bathrooms. My mother might have wondered why hers did not.

Sometimes the Bible is taken out of context to justify domestic violence. Perhaps they quote Ephesians 5:22-24 about wives being subject to their husbands: "Wives, be subject to your husbands as you are to the Lord. For the husband is the head of the wife just as Christ is the head of the church, the body of which he is the Savior. Just as the church is subject to Christ, so also wives ought to be, in everything, to their husbands."

That passage applies to a different context of another age, much like the verses in the following chapter which implore slaves to "obey your earthly masters with fear and trembling." These verses were written when everyone believed that the sun and planets revolved around us. Since that time, our understanding of our physical world has changed, as has our social world's understanding that women are not subservient, people of color cannot be considered as property, gay people are not a mistake, and one person may not control another because of gender, race, sexual orientation, or any other reason.

Abuse is not your fault, it is not God's will, and it is not punishment. Sometimes an abused person may see their suffering as just punishment for a past deed. Or, they may see their abuse as God's will, as a part of God's plan for their life, or God's way of teaching them a lesson. Abuse does not occur because God is mad at you. God, who sheds the gift of grace over all, does not cause bad things to happen to people. All people are God's beloved children. A loving Parent would never consider abuse as a way to punish or teach a lesson. God does not work like that. The loving and compassionate God wants for you that which is best in your life.

Abuse is not your fault. Abuse does not happen to you because you did something bad. Do not blame yourself. Being abused is not a failure of your character or your faith. Even if you care for the person who hurts you, they are the one doing wrong. Not you. Abuse is not because you are to blame, even if someone tells you that you are. Abuse is not a consequence of poor choices, being stupid, a bad attitude, or not being able to get your act together.

You have rights: You have a right to a home without constant conflict. You have a right to be you and to be free. You have a right to life, liberty, and the pursuit of happiness. You have a right to your own privacy. You have a right to your dignity and your reputation. You have a right to say no. You have the right to be safe, physically and emotionally.

A "Me Too" movement is needed for those who suffer from abusive relationships, to focus the spotlight publicly on anyone who takes advantage of another and abuses their rights and freedoms. It is too late to help my mother, who died too soon from what seems to me the stress caused by an abusive relationship. I pray for a movement to give courage to others who may be reluctant to seek the help they need to break out of a trap which can feel like there is no way out.

Jesus brought the world a new way of seeing love. The New Testament word for love is agape, which can mean to desire that which is in the highest and best interest of the other. If someone hurts another, whether by hitting or by controlling them emotionally, that is not seeking what is truly best for the person. There is no way that behavior can be described as love. That is abuse. It is violence, even if someone does not hit you physically. It is a violation of covenant between two people.

Do not give up on your faith. Trust that God is with you in your worst of times. To the abused, it can appear like there is no hope, no way out. It is a dark time. The literal translation of the phrase in Psalm 23:4 is *"the valley of dark shadows."* For people who are abused, that may be the most comforting message in the Bible. In the valley, you are not alone: *"Yea, though I walk through the valley of dark shadows, I will fear no evil. For thou art with me."* Some of God's sheep suffer abuse. God leaves the flock to go and be with them in their darkest shadows of brokenness, for they need the compassionate touch of the Shepherd so very much.

                                        Published in The Christian Citizen October 15, 2018

The social justice Christmas carol

John Sullivan Dwight of Boston was a social activist in the 1800s. He graduated from Harvard College and Harvard University Divinity School and became a pastor in Northampton, Massachusetts. As an ardent abolitionist during the century marked by the Civil War, the pulpit could have become a launching pad for John's advocacy on behalf of the oppressed. Except for one thing. John Dwight suffered from a queasy stomach. Every time he stood up before his congregation, he grew sick. Many a pastor has suffered from Sunday morning stomach, although pastors do not talk about it much. Perhaps it is brought on by the anxiety of public speaking, which today ranks as a top fear of people in the United States. In John's case, his panic attacks magnified to the point that he needed to find another occupation.

Leaving the pastoral ministry, John launched "Dwight's Journal of Music," a weekly periodical that became one of the most respected and influential such periodicals in the country. He edited the journal for thirty years.

Of all the things John Dwight might have been known for, one towered above all others: a Christmas carol he published in his journal in the mid 1800s. It was written by a local commissionaire of wines in a small French village, Placide Cappeau. Cappeau was not known to be a person of faith, yet he wrote the poem *"Minuit, chrétiens"* at the request of the parish priest for the dedication of the church's renovated organ. For the tune, Cappeau turned to his Jewish friend Adolphe Charles Adam, who composed the tune *"Cantique de Noël."* The people of France loved it. The church didn't and banned it, saying it was "unfit for church services because of its lack of musical taste and its 'total absence of the spirit of religion.'" In the church's view, the carol was not spiritual enough, perhaps because of who wrote it and composed it. The people of France apparently didn't get the memo, because they continued to sing it and love it and no one was going to take it away from them.

John Dwight translated the carol into English and published it in "Dwight's Journal of Music" under the title *"O Holy Night."*

O Holy Night! The stars are brightly shining,
It is the night of the dear Savior's birth.
Long lay the world in sin and error pining.
Till He appeared and the soul felt its worth.
A thrill of hope the weary world rejoices,
For yonder breaks a new and glorious morn.

Fall on your knees! Oh, hear the angel voices!
O night divine, the night when Christ was born;
O night, O Holy Night , O night divine!
O night, O Holy Night , O night divine!

The hymn's verse which grabbed him and shook him by the shoulders spoke directly to his passion for advocating on behalf of the oppressed:

Truly he taught us to love one another;
his law is love and his gospel is peace.
Chains shall he break, for the slave is our brother;
and in his name all oppression shall cease.

The best songs lead us into the worship of God and also challenge us to do something for others, as "O Holy Night" does so well. It invites us to worship, to "fall on your knees! O hear the angel voices!" Then, there is a time to get up from our knees and do something, because God needs everyday Christians in the work for social justice, and to stand with and speak for our brothers and sisters who are oppressed. The slave or anyone who is oppressed is our brother and our sister. God's world is a world without borders, fences or walls, so we are beckoned to work for freedom from oppression for all people in our land or in faraway lands. God needs us to favor those who are oppressed. Should the oppressed become free and themselves become oppressors, God needs us to favor the new oppressed.

"Those who oppress the poor insult their Maker, but those who are kind to the needy honor him," says Proverbs 14:31 (NRSV). We only sing "O Holy Night" once a year. Yet may this social justice Christmas carol call forth our determination and our action, in God's name, that all oppression shall cease. The nature and characteristics of those who are oppressed change over time, but the need continues for God's people of faith to serve God as abolitionists of oppression. May we honor God by being kind to those who are oppressed.

Published in <u>The Christian Citizen</u> December 20, 2018

Martin Luther King Jr. Day:
A good day to think about patriotism

I like thinking about patriotism on Martin Luther King Jr. Day. King was one of our greatest patriots and provided leadership far ahead of his times. He came out early against the Vietnam war as an unjust, evil, and futile war. That was well before it was popular to oppose the war and was a bold, courageous act, which paved the way for others to follow. From the pulpit of the Ebenezer Baptist Church in Atlanta, on April 30, 1967, King delivered his famous sermon, "Why I Am Opposed to the War in Vietnam." He said, "But the day has passed for superficial patriotism. He who lives with untruth lives in spiritual slavery. Freedom is still the bonus we receive for knowing the truth. 'Ye shall know the truth,' says Jesus, 'and the truth shall set you free'."

I do not care for thinking about patriotism on the national holidays. Patriotism, as exemplified by Dr. King, thinks evaluatively about one's country in light of its best values, including the attempt to correct it when it's in error and fix it when it is broken. Yet especially on our national patriotic holidays, too often our churches promote nationalism—the uncritical support of one's nation regardless of its moral, truthful or political bearing. I attended a worship service on a national holiday. The service, designed to lead worshippers into an encounter with the Divine, began with the presentation of the American flag by the Scouts, followed by a parade of men in old military uniforms. Next came the Pledge of Allegiance, standing up. This scene likely plays out in congregations throughout the land. The pastor did his best to encourage critical thinking, but this kind of nationalism makes it feel unpatriotic to question, to consider alternative ways of thinking, or to criticize these practices.

Careful here. I can imagine my beloved mother saying "Johnny, we must honor our boys who sacrificed so much for their country." She would have stood for the pledge and belted out the national hymns with pride and gusto. And yet, she raised me in an American Baptist church less than six miles from where Martin Luther King, Jr. attended Crozer Theological Seminary. Some of my pastors were his classmates. I was raised in that church to think globally, for God so loved the world (*cosmos* is the Greek word in this verse).

I grew up hearing "thou shalt not kill" and "love your enemies" and "blessed are the peacemakers." The church taught me to think, to consider implications of attitudes and behavior, and to recognize that, like the disciples, there is a time to obey God rather than humans, even if that calls for civil disobedience. This church modeled that Christians are to be champions for the human race, without borders, boundaries or walls. Whether from across the avenue or from Central America, the one in need was my neighbor. I knew that part of my allowance went to helping people in faraway countries. Essayist William Hazlitt said "The love of liberty is the love of others. The love of power is the love of ourselves." Because we were raised to love others, all others, the consequence is that we learned to love liberty. Two words summarize how I was raised in that American Baptist church: it was centered upon love and forgiveness.

In the midst of the Vietnam war, I received a piece of mail from the Selective Service System that began with the word "Greetings!" along with the invitation to report for a physical, to prepare to be drafted into the army. Because I was raised to think critically and evaluatively, I tried to reconcile the Christian teachings of my church with the potential of being drafted. If I stepped across the line, I would be required to carry out orders, even if that meant to kill another human being. What if I was ordered to kill another human, a husband or a father, for a war which one of my heroes called "unjust, evil, and futile"? It did not reconcile. And so I decided that I would reject the invitation and pay whatever price was needed. I was prepared to become a conscientious objector—and then a new lottery of draft numbers was initiated and I ended up with a high number. I was excused, but I would have been ready and willing to pay the price.

Decades later, Martin Luther King Jr.'s words still deeply resonate with me: "…the day has passed for superficial patriotism. He who lives with untruth lives in spiritual slavery." Please, please, please let our nation think critically and evaluatively about the growing number of untruths proffered in our time, even from the highest offices. If we do not, we shall be bound in spiritual slavery. When I attend a service designed for the worship of God and instead, I experience an exercise in the deification of nationalism, I am distraught and cannot help but think that spiritual slavery is occurring before our eyes.

I truly want to be patriotic. I listen to The Sound of Music's "Edelweiss, Edelweiss, Bless my homeland forever" and I long to sing that about the United States of America. I love the patriotism of Ralph Waldo Emerson, who said "When a whole nation is roaring patriotism at the top of its voice, I am fain to explore the cleanness of its hands and purity of its heart." I dislike the patriotism described by George Bernard Shaw: "Patriotism is, fundamentally, a conviction that a particular country is superior to all others because you were born in it." I can easily reconcile my church's teachings with the patriotic voice from Malcolm Little (also known as Malcolm X): "You're not supposed to be so blind with patriotism that you can't face reality. Wrong is wrong, no matter who does it or who says it." There are some wrong things going on in our country today, inconsistent with the teachings of Jesus of Nazareth. Thinking Christians must not surrender their sense of patriotism and global *agape* (the Greek word for love) to an uncritical devotion to nationalism.

I pretty much avoid going to church on those national patriotic holidays, which are hardly holy days. And yet, on Martin Luther King, Jr. Day – a national holiday which I am proud to celebrate – I like to think about the best of patriotism, how he was a patriot and leader ahead of his time, and to use this day to celebrate my citizenship in the Kingdom of God and in the United States of America.

Published in <u>The Christian Citizen</u> January 17, 2019

The day they hid the Liberty Bell

"Proclaim liberty throughout all the land unto all the inhabitants thereof." (Leviticus 25:10 KJV).

A precious sketch for a painting hangs in my home depicting the day they moved the Liberty Bell from Philadelphia to hide it under the floor of the Old Zion Reformed Church in Allentown, Pennsylvania, where it remained until June 27, 1778. The painting is by Philadelphia-area artist Donald Cleveland Taber (1895-1981), my wife's beloved grandfather. The church, now known as the Zion's Reformed United Church of Christ, has the unique website of libertybellchurch.org and the church hosts the Liberty Bell Museum.

I was born in Philadelphia and like every school kid, our yellow buses delivered us on field trips to Independence Hall where we viewed the Liberty Bell. The bell did not always sit protected behind a bulletproof glass chamber. With my finger, I have traced the crack in the bell, perhaps reminding us always that freedom and liberty is a fragile blessing. With my knuckles, I have rapped the Liberty Bell to hear the ring of freedom. Let freedom ring throughout our land. My eyes were captivated by the quote on the top of the Liberty Bell, which bears the inscription from Leviticus 25:10: "Proclaim liberty throughout all the land unto all the inhabitants thereof."

After our encounter with the bell and a tour of Independence Hall, we were escorted to the next most important site: the store! It was there I bought a mock parchment replica of the Declaration of Independence with its soaring language of freedom for all: "We hold these truths to be self-evident, that all men are created equal, that they are endowed by their Creator with certain unalienable Rights, that among these are Life, Liberty and the pursuit of Happiness." Even in those days, a generation before inclusive language, I understood that *men* meant all women, children and men. And I understood that the word *all* contained no exceptions.

In June 1753, the bell was hung in the old wooden steeple of the State House, erected on top of the brick tower. It was in use while the Continental Congress was in session in the State House, it rang out in defiance of British tax and trade restrictions, and it proclaimed the Boston Tea Party and the first public reading of the Declaration of Independence.

The website for the Liberty Bell Shrine in Allentown explains: "At the signing of the Declaration of Independence, the bell of Independence Hall rang to proclaim liberty throughout the land… But a year later things were going badly for Washington and the patriots. Philadelphia was about to fall into enemy hands. The British were running low on ammunition, and it was known that they would melt the city's church bells for musket and cannon balls. The nation's Executive Council decided to send the bells to the village of Northampton, now known as Allentown. A train of 700 wagons was organized to carry military stores to Bethlehem. The Liberty Bell was aboard one of these wagons… After its arrival at Bethlehem, the bells were hauled to Northampton, where they were hidden under the floor of Old Zion Reformed Church, where they remained until the British evacuated Philadelphia. The Liberty Bell and church bells were then restored to their proper places."

The painting by Donald Cleveland Taber depicts the moving of the Liberty Bell on the way to its hiding place at the Old Zion Reformed Church. The nation's beloved and precious symbol of liberty, flawed as it may be, is a steadfast and bold reminder of the word "all." "Proclaim liberty throughout all the land unto all the inhabitants thereof." The intent of American liberty was always directed to all, although our practices, like the bell, contain some cracks in them. There are people who have been—and some who still are—excluded from this word "all." In that, our nation has failed and has sinned. "Injustice anywhere is a threat to justice everywhere," wrote Martin Luther King, Jr. in his Letter from Birmingham Jail. We as people of faith are called and compelled to serve as ambassadors for justice everywhere and to all.

The Liberty Bell extends its palms up and open arms message to all. At a time when our nation's polarization divides opinions about who is welcome and who is not, and when America's leaders at the highest levels close borders, build walls and contradict the welcome offered by the words on the baseplate of our nation's Statue of Liberty, we need once again to hear the Liberty Bell's ring of liberty with an emphasis on the word "*all*."

It's hard to grow up visiting the Liberty Bell, just blocks from where Betsy Ross pieced together America's first flag, and not feel a sense of national pride and patriotism. And yet, patriotism has an ugly side to it, when it is blind, deaf, dumb, closed-minded and unwelcoming. I confess a stomach-turning discomfort when I witness giant-sized American flags waving from car dealers, flag presentation ceremonies in worship services or the pseudo-patriotism of political rallies enveloped in red, white and blue. But they may not co-opt a true sense of patriotism away from me, or from the intent of the Liberty Bell's ring of freedom.

"True patriotism hates injustice in its own land more than anywhere else," goes a quote attributed to Clarence Darrow. Injustice occurs when the word "*all*" contains exceptions, even those hidden beneath the surface of civility. That injustice is worthy to be hated, when liberty excludes Mexicans, Muslims, Medicare recipients, LGBTQ people, those with a skin pigment different than yours, those who are differently abled, or those who exercise their freedom to disagree with or to protest against injustice.

Let us, true patriots, accept the call from Leviticus and from Philadelphia to be proclaimers of liberty throughout all the land unto all the inhabitants. Let us be true to the word "*all*." Let us labor so that the ring of freedom need never again to be hidden under the floorboards.

Published in <u>The Christian Citizen</u> February 22, 2019

Probing questions in Lent

On Easter Sunday, church attendance surges to overflowing. Longtime members whisper to one another how wonderful it would be if every Sunday could be like Easter. Additional services must be added in some congregations to hold all those who come to worship, to praise and to glorify God. The Easter message: "He is not here. He is risen!"

It can be an emotional Sunday. If the church were to ask and to listen to its people, it might hear that a number of its most devout members have some confusion, questions or doubt about Easter. When do those members raise their questions and connect with others in conversation about the resurrection of Jesus of Nazareth? Certainly not on Easter Sunday. And so, one of the best times to consider the questions of the curious is during Lent, when thinking people of faith can wonder and converse about the meaning of Easter.

One of most challenging questions pondered by thinking Christians is: Was it a physical resurrection from the dead? A longtime church member told how she has a hard time with Easter because she does not really believe in the physical resurrection of Jesus. The Easter message proclaims "He is not here. He is risen!" There may be devout and faithful people in your congregation who love God and follow Jesus but may question if it was a physical resurrection. Is this question a threat? Do you think it might weaken your faith to even consider this question? Do you think God would be upset if people question traditional or orthodox beliefs?

What you think about Jesus is called your "Christology." Do you think of Jesus as God or as man or as both? Was he more one than the other? Imagine it on a scale of one to ten.

At the highest end, the ten, the view of Christology holds that Jesus, the Christ, is 100% God. This is the highest Christology which believes that Jesus was not man but was God in a man's body. "The Father and I are one," Jesus said in John 10:30 (NRSV). Both are equally God.

Later Jesus told the disciples "Whoever has seen me has seen the Father." (John 14:9 NRSV). A ten on the scale holds that Jesus is purely divine and not human. Jesus is God.

On the other end, the one on the scale, the view of Christology holds that Jesus is 100% man. This view believes that he was the son of God or a son of God because he told the truth about God. Jesus got it right better than anyone. He had an inspired view of who God is and what God is like. This view recognizes that in his teachings, Jesus of Nazareth did not point to himself, but he pointed to God. He did not say pray like this: "Our Jesus who art in heaven." He did not propose that the greatest commandment was "To love the Lord your Jesus with all your heart, mind, soul, and might." He did not encourage his followers to "Seek first the Kingdom of Jesus." He did not come to preach the good news of the kingdom of Jesus. It's not about me, Jesus would have said. It's about God. That is what is really important, is it not? So the low end of the Christology scale perceives a Christ who was the son of God, anointed by God, sent, inspired, pointing always to God. A man, teaching a way of life of love and forgiveness, the God-like way to live, the very best way for humans to live. Jesus is human.

In between, around the five on the scale, the view of Christology sees Jesus as possessing a dual nature, being both human and divine. Here Jesus is the Word become flesh: "And the Word became flesh and dwelt among us…" (John 1:14 NKJV). Jesus is God, the second person of the Trinity. And Jesus is man, who suffered like us. He understands what we go through for he himself went through it. The reason there are two candles on many altars is to symbolize the two natures of Jesus: human and divine. Man and God. Both.

It is possible that in many congregations there exist people on every mark of that one-to-ten scale. The best gathering of God's people is inclusive, embracing every person with all of their beliefs, doubts, warts and all. In God-like congregations, you can be a two, four, six, eight, or ten and still be a member of the Christian church. There is room for all.

It is possible that you may wake up on different days and find yourself at a different place on the scale. You might be all over the place. Some days you wake up and you are a ten, believing that Jesus is God, that he and the Father are one. Other days you wake up and perhaps you are a one, believing that what Jesus taught about God is what is important. Most days, perhaps, you fall in the four to six range.

So which is correct? No one can tell you which number is exactly right, but anyone who insists that you must believe a certain way and be a specific number is wrong. No one can tell you where you must fall on the scale. You are just as welcome to your understanding of the nature of Christ and his resurrection. Wherever you fall on the scale, you can sing those Easter hymns however you want and still be welcome, included and valued. That kind of extravagant welcome seems downright God-like. Trying our best to be God-like is one million times more important than where a person falls on the belief-o-meter scale. God accepts and loves you as you are. Go and do likewise: accept others the same way, wherever they fall on the scale.

Our lives are rooted in belief, as Jesus taught "Blessed are those who have not seen and yet have come to believe" (John 20:29 NRSV). We are all still a work in progress, "coming" to believe. And yet, never be afraid of the quest for truth. God has nothing to fear from your search for truth or from your curiosity. And Jesus, called *Rabboni* or teacher by those who knew him best, could not be imagined to be insulted by a student who raises hard questions or who is curious. That is not the nature of a master teacher.

                                        Published in The Christian Citizen March 21, 2019

Just when is the light supposed to break forth like the dawn?

"Then your light shall break forth like the dawn, and your healing shall spring up quickly; your vindicator shall go before you, the glory of the Lord shall be your rear guard."
(Isaiah 58:8 NRSV)

As I was leaving a visit with my parishioner, Muriel, and standing in the doorway, she said "When I watch TV news, it feels like evil is winning." That caught me off guard. How do you discuss hours' worth of systematic theology while you are buttoning up your coat? But I had to answer with something. So, I responded with Jesus' I AM statement from the Gospel of John: "I am the light of the world. Whoever follows me will never walk in darkness but will have the light of life." (John 8:12 NRSV). I tried to reassure Muriel that no matter how bleak things appear, the darkness will not overcome the light. Now, years later, I think my best intentions were misguided. I think I was wrong. What are we to say when leaders of a nation, society or culture seem to promote darkness rather than light?

Today in the United States we experience a president who behaves less maturely than a five-year-old, a Supreme Court tilting so far to starboard that it could capsize, and a Congress which is held in lower respect than almost any other occupation, although there may be some new hope on the horizon. Our planet is threatened by human-caused climate change, yet many in our top leadership positions deny science and assign responsibility for the henhouse to foxes. Many citizens feel so helpless, harassed or depressed that they cannot stand to watch the TV news anymore. Perhaps Muriel was correct: it feels like evil is winning.

Like John, the prophet Isaiah proclaimed, "Then your light shall break forth like the dawn, and your healing shall spring up quickly." Light may have eventually dawned years after the Holocaust or South Africa's apartheid, but that gave small comfort to those who suffered tragic loss, pain or death. For a long time, darkness prevailed—and there are signs today of a pervasive evil in our land.

The hundreds and maybe thousands of children dragged away by the U.S. government from their migrating parents seeking to fall into the arms of the Statue of Liberty may find little relief from words about darkness not overcoming the light. The millions cascading down out of the middle class while the upper one percent increases their wealth geometrically may rightly wonder just when is the light supposed to break forth? Perhaps not in time to do them any good.

Consider when Jesus spoke these words about being the light of the world and how "Whoever follows me will never walk in darkness but will have the light of life." When Jesus entered the world, an evil-minded Herod ordered all young children to be killed in order to hopefully eliminate Jesus. "When Herod saw that he had been tricked by the wise men, he was infuriated, and he sent and killed all the children in and around Bethlehem who were two years old or under, according to the time that he had learned from the wise men." (Matthew 2:16 NRSV). This is the dark side to Christmas which rarely, if ever, makes it into the annual Christmas pageant. Thirty-three years later, leaders of darkness sought and obtained Jesus' death. How would you explain to someone that the Light of the World was sent by God to our planet, and we killed him? You couldn't blame the earliest followers of Jesus for questioning just when the light is supposed to break forth like the dawn.

When Jesus refers to being the light, perhaps he is not applying this to political, social or cultural experience but to something else. But what? He speaks in metaphor, uses figures of speech and frequently employs Middle Eastern teaching techniques like hyperbole, parallelism, patterns and parable. How are we to understand? Perhaps when Jesus spoke about the darkness not overcoming the light, he was not speaking about a nation's politics or governance.

Jesus came into the world to bring us the good news and to teach us the truth about God. That is the light. When John began his gospel, he talked about the mind of God becoming flesh and dwelling among us to enlighten us. "The true light, which enlightens everyone, was coming into the world." (John 1:9 NRSV).

When Jesus said, "Whoever follows me will never walk in darkness but will have the light of life," notice the pronoun: *whoever*. This is personal. This applies to you, me and anyone who follows him. Our following him, which is good news, is not likely to be shown on TV news. It is the nature of TV news for viewers to witness more darkness than light. It is also the nature of TV news to focus disproportionately on politics and politicians. Jesus was speaking personally: *whoever follows me*. He was not speaking politically or culturally. He did not say that when the light of the world arrives, our politics and society will change dramatically for the better. In many cases, it has not. However, when the light of the world arrives, the light has the potential to change people, and people have the potential to change society and culture for good. The goal for people of faith is not to make our nation great again, but to make our nation good again. Therefore, how extraordinarily critical it is for followers of Jesus to let their lights shine, especially in the darkest of places and at the darkest of times. A critical mass of followers who reflect God's radiated light become a model and a warm glow when it is needed most. They serve as an example of the best of people aspiring to the goals of love, joy, peace, patience, kindness, goodness, faithfulness, gentleness and self-control – the fruit of the spirit.

Do not let the TV news or even national leadership going in the wrong direction draw you into darkness. Welcome into your soul the light of The Great I AM and trust that "Whoever follows me will never walk in darkness but will have the light of life."

Published in The Christian Citizen March 26, 2019

The quietest, loneliest and most painful illness

"Why are you cast down, O my soul, and why are you disquieted within me? Hope in God..." (Psalm 42:11)

Mental Health Awareness? Those who suffer from mental health issues are so aware that there is hardly a moment of the day when it does not dominate their thoughts. For roughly 20 percent of the American population (over 46 million people), mental illness can be a living hell for them, their caregivers, family and friends.

Mental illness has touched my family, and perhaps yours has experienced it too. The list of celebrities, athletes, writers, artists, professionals, and everyday people who have experienced it seems endless. Do a quick internet search for famous people with mental illness to discover many others who share this dark valley. In history, those who may have had a mental health condition include Abraham Lincoln, Ludwig van Beethoven, Michelangelo, Charles Dickens, Charles Darwin, Winston Churchill, Leo Tolstoy, and Isaac Newton.

It is the loneliest of diseases. Mental illness – like depression, bipolar disorder, anxiety, and panic disorder – touches so many lives. It does not care about how much education you have, how well raised you were, how much money you've got, how successful you've been, what kind of person you are, or where you go to church.

It is the quietest of illnesses. Sometimes we do not know we have it. Or, we do not acknowledge it. We do not talk about it much. We do not want to. Few people know or understand. Yet the hurting is profound, confusing, and lonely.

If you have cared for a member of your family or a friend who suffers from mental illness, you have probably considered that any physical illness seems preferable to a mental illness. With a physical illness, people visit, they send cards, bring meals, offer prayers, and demonstrate their care, support and attention.

But with a mental illness, you do not know what is happening, where it is going, and you are not completely sure that maybe it is not something you did. What will people think? And so, you build walls and keep it closed up inside, where it is so very lonely.

Thankfully the stigma is declining, but it is still present. The stigma is one of the greatest enemies to mental health awareness. Stigma is an illness too. Let us, people of God, pledge ourselves to slaying that awful giant of stigma. Wherever we can, let us become healers of this illness so that all God's sheep may enjoy an abundant life.

Consider three realities about mental illness.

First, mental illness is a disease, not a failure of character and not a failure of faith. Scientists are discovering that brain disorders are largely a matter of genetics and biochemistry. Eric Kandel, MD, a Nobel Prize laureate and professor of brain science at Columbia University, believes it's all about biology. "All mental processes are brain processes, and therefore all disorders of mental functioning are biological diseases," he says. "The brain is the organ of the mind. Where else could mental illness be if not in the brain?" Mental illness is a disease. It is not your fault. You did not do anything wrong. It is not a result of your upbringing. It is not a consequence of poor choices, being stupid, a bad attitude, or not being able to get your act together. Mental illness is not a failure of your faith. The fact that you cannot pull yourself out of the hole is not a reflection of your weakness. When you pray to get better and you do not, it is not a sign that God does not care. When you have deep, dark thoughts that you cannot tell anyone about, it is not because you did something bad or because you are a bad person. God is not mad at you. God is not trying to teach you a lesson. God is not trying to punish you. The loving Parent that Jesus taught about does not work that way.

Second, mental illness can be managed. It might not get cured, but it can become managed. Through new discoveries in therapies and prescription drugs, many people with mental illness are able to live satisfying, effective, successful, and even happy lives. There is hope. With help, life can become not only possible but pleasurable. And yet, some with mental illness do not seek help, for a number of reasons. There is denial.

Some believe that they are quite independent and they will fix what is broken themselves. Some resist admitting that they have a problem that needs help. Some have a lack of hope in the mental health profession. Some wonder if the path to recovery is paved with unending medical bills. Not all insurance policies cover mental illness, and most that do only cover a part. And yet, many with mental illnesses have sought professional help and they are managing well. That is one of the keys: understanding that you do not necessarily get rid of it, but you learn to manage. There is hope and there is help. Mental illness can benefit significantly if treated.

Third, what works with regular depression may not work with clinical depression. Most people get depressed. These folks tell themselves, "Come on, pick yourself up. Bolster your attitude. Get a life. Change your attitude. You can do it." Clinically depressed people may try to say those things too, but nothing happens. Then, they may blame themselves or feel that their faith is too weak or they just figure that faith does not work. Faith does not banish clinical depression, any more than it banishes cancer, canker sores or cataracts. "You can't 'pray away' a mental health condition," notes the National Alliance on Mental Illness. So do not blame yourself or God when prayers, hymns, sermons, scriptures, or encouraging friends do not seem to change your mood. Mental illness is a chemical imbalance in your insides, it is a disease, and it is one that can often be treated.

Some of God's sheep have a mental illness—about one out of five. We understand so little about it. In many ways, we are still in the dark ages. Mental illness is a quiet, lonely, and dark valley. Psalm 23 says: "Even though I walk through the darkest valley, I fear no evil; for you are with me" (Psalm 23:4 NRSV). For people with a mental illness, that may be one of the most important messages in the Bible: you are not alone.

Published in <u>The Christian Citizen</u> week of April 17, 2019

About the Author

John Zehring has served United Church of Christ congregations for more than twenty years as Senior Pastor in Massachusetts (Andover), Rhode Island (Kingston), Maine (Augusta) and as an Interim Pastor in Massachusetts (Arlington, Harvard). Prior to parish ministry, he served as a vice president and teacher at colleges, universities, and a theological seminary for more than two decades. He is the author of more than forty books and eBooks. Rev. Zehring graduated from Eastern University and holds graduate degrees from Princeton Theological Seminary, Rider University, and the Earlham School of Religion.

Books by John Zehring

Essays on Justice, Goodness and Faith: Volume 1. 2019

Majestic is Thy Name: Devotions from the Psalms. 2019.

Treasures from Proverbs: GEMS for You from the Book of Proverbs. 2018.

Treasures from Rome: GEMS for You from the Epistle to the Romans. 2018.

Get Your Church Ready to Grow: A Guide to Building Attendance & Participation. 2018.

Beyond Stewardship: A Church Guide to Generous Giving Campaigns. 2016.

Asking for Campaign Support: A Guide for Church Volunteers. 2018.

Clergy Quick Guide to Encouraging Leaders and Staff. Also… evaluating staff and evaluating yourself. 2017.

Hard Sayings of Jesus: Discussions for Curious Christians. 2017.

Clergy Quick Guide to Time Management. 2017.

Pastoral Leadership and Church Administration. 2017.

Miracles? Discussions for Curious Christians about Jesus' Miracles. 2018.

Treasures from James: GEMS for You from the Epistle of James. 2017.

Eulogies, Introductions and Special Occasion Speeches: Tips for When You Are Asked to Speak Well of Another. 2017.

Treasures from Galatia: GEMS for You from the Epistle to the Galatians. 2017.

Lent Discussions for Curious Christians: Conversations in the Purple Season. 2017.

Favorite Parables from Jesus of Nazareth. 2016.

Anxious? A Booklet of Bible Verses for When You Feel Anxious. 2016.

Clergy Guide to Sermon Preparation: Including 40 Sermon Ideas and Outlines. 2015.

Mount Up with Wings: Renew Your Strength. 2015.

Jesus' Sermon on the Mount: Matthew 5, 6 and 7. 2015.

Visiting on Behalf of Your Church: A Guide for Deacons, Care Teams and Those Who Visit. 2015.

The One Minute Beatitude: A Brief Review of Jesus' Beatitudes. 2015.

Seven Mantras to Shape Your Day: Bible Verses to Improve How You See Things. 2015.

Psalm 23: An Everyday Psalm. 2015.

By the Golden Rule. Torture is Always Wrong. 2014.

Public Speaking for Executives. Leaders & Managers. 2014.

Clergy Guide to Making Visits. 2014.

Clergy Public Speaking Guide: Improve What You Already Do Well. 2014.

Clergy Negotiating Guide: Don't Sell Yourself Short. 2014.

Treasures from Philippi: GEMS for You from the Epistle to the Philippians. 2014.

What the Bible Says About Homosexuality: A Bible Study for Progressive People of Faith. 2014.

Did He Hit Her? A Compassionate Christian Response to Abusive Relationships. 2014.

To Know God Better And To Love God More: Messages for Your Spiritual Journey. 2014.

You Can Run A Capital Campaign: A Guide for Church Leaders. 1990.

Work Smarter -- Not Harder: A Manual for Development Officers. 1986.

WORKING SMART: The Handbook for New Managers. 1985.

Careers in State and Local Government. 1980.

Preparing for W*O*R*K. 1981.

Making Your Life Count. 1980.

IMPLICATIONS: Case Studies for Ethical and Spiritual Development. 1980.

Get Your Career In Gear: How To Find Or Change Your Lifework. 1976.

Made in the USA
Middletown, DE
19 April 2019